Praise for Chip Helm and his information-packed, practical, and essential new book...

"Chip Helm is relatively unique as a visiting instructor in the college classroom. He is both inspirational and instructive as it relates to the sales profession. He has always been met with considerable student enthusiasm over the last few years in my classes."

—**Dick Canada**, Founder for the Center for Global Sales Leadership and Marketing Professor, Kelley School of Business, Indiana University, Bloomington, IN

"Each semester I have the good fortune to have Chip Helm talk to my undergraduate and MBA students. Chip brings over 30 years of sales and sales management experience into the classroom. Whether Chip talks about "Branding Yourself" or his "Five Steps to Sales Success," the students come away with intuitive and actionable insights into selling themselves or a product. Chip's high-energy presentations are contagious as he captivates his audience with humor and outstanding sales knowledge."

—**Ramon A. Avila**, George and Frances Ball Distinguished Professor of Marketing, Ball State University, Muncie, IN

"Chip Helm is someone who has a strong emotional empathy that resonates with everyone. He has generously given his personal time to speak at collegiate sales club meetings and has shared his story and experiences from working at Cook Medical for 32 years. He encourages others to succeed and strongly believes that each individual will find their own unique way to accomplish great things in life."

—**Maddie DuBois**, President of Sales Club at Kelley School of Business

D1234682

"Thanks Chip! Appreciate all the direction and mentorship you have given me over the last 8 years. I've said it before, I'll never stop calling you for suggestions and help throughout my career."

—**Greg Toplitz**, Manager, HCP Education and Development, Medical Education (Americas), *Cook Medical*

"Chip Helm is as passionate about sales as anyone I've ever met. With an extensive and impressive history in his time at Cook Medical, Chip Helm embodies the ideal, personable salesman. As a sophomore in the Kelley School of Business, I am constantly looking to further develop my professional sales skills. With Chip's aid and mentorship, he has provided me a glimpse of what it is like to be a professional in the world of sales, and I am glad to have a relationship with him."

—**Adam Scheck**, IU Kelley School of Business – 2020, Marketing & Professional Sales Major

"It's always a grand day when you come to Kelley to guest lecture – seriously! We are so appreciative of your insight and 'real world' perspective in the classroom as well as when you participate in various other sales activities. The center's corporate partners are critical to our success, and your role is instrumental in supporting our sales mission. We could not exist without Cook's generosity and belief in what we do, and we are so grateful for your positive energy, time, and support."

—**Sonya Dunigan**, Assistant Director, Center for Global Sales Leadership, Indiana University, Kelley School of Business

"My experience with Chip Helm was hearing him give a talk to one of my college classes during my junior year. The class discussed consultative selling, and Chip's insight was crucial. He creates little ounces of wisdom called "Chipisms" which are off-the-cuff bits of insight into both selling and life. Some mentioned during my class period were, "We're all in sales;" "You need a goal, and your goal can change;" "You have to decide what you want to do in life;" "Use what you've got to your advantage." The most impactful "Chipism" to me was, "You need a goal, and your goal can change." Previously in my life, I tend to shy away from specific goals, and rather just do the best I can because I didn't want to fail reaching my goal. This message inspired me to not view goals as scary or unreachable, but rather my accomplice in becoming a better person, and achieving what I want in my life."

"He also outlines the *5 Truths of a Sale* which are 'Follow up;' 'Never give up on a customer;' 'Relationships;' 'Networking;' and 'Passion.' If you have these five components on the forefront in your mind when approaching a sale, you will ultimately find success. Maybe not the first time, but with persistence and hard work, you will eventually create a successful selling environment."

—**Erin Weber**, Student Center for Global Sales Leadership
Kelly School of Business

"Chip is a fantastic source for college students, recent graduates, and others new to the world of sales. He combines a sincere desire to help and inform with a quick wit, dry sense of humor, and real-world talk Chip is repeatedly asked for and requested to speak at collegiate employer panels across Indiana. Chip is someone who will willingly stay after and speak to as many students individually as needed, get the entire audience laughing at a story, or be blunt and tell them honest to goodness truth about expectations out in the 'real world.' When Chip is talking, all eyes are riveted and barely a blink happens. He is a fantastic partner to Indiana State University and our students are better due to his continued presence working with them."

—**Kyle Harris**, M.S., CDF, Assistant Director, Career Center,
Liaison to Bayh College of Education,
Liaison to Scott College of Business, Indiana State University

"Humility is a word that most people do not associate with career professionals and salespeople. But that is exactly what struck me about the book by Chip Helm, where he unequivocally bats for humility as a key character requisite for people to succeed in their careers. His conviction that humility can help professionals improve their work-life balance is a very engaging and interesting concept, one that professionals forget sometimes."

"I thought the talk about Personal Branding was eye-opening. I know that I need to watch what I post on social media, but it was a different twist when I actually thought what my personal brand was. The tip you gave about asking other people what they thought of me was something I never thought of before. It was shocking/refreshing hearing about your struggles in the business world. Everyone normally talks about the success they had but never touch on the hard times in their lives. I loved the energy and enthusiasm so early in the morning. You really did a good job including everyone in the conversation. I think it is a good idea having people use name tags because you got people to volunteer speaking who normally would not talk. I am very interested in reading your new book."

—**Shannon Eden**, Student, Kelly School of Business,

"Recently, I had Chip Helm come and share his thoughts on the concepts of personal branding and his take on the '5 Truths of Sales.' Not only did the students enjoy his presentation, they actually ended up getting a lot of useful tips/tricks about how they could build and maintain their personal brands, while being successful in sales. I am really looking forward to having Chip back in front of my students in the next semester."

—**Deva Rangarajan, Ph.D.** Associate Professor of Marketing, Associate Director of the Center for Professional Selling, Miller College of Business

Everyday Sales Wisdom
for Your Life & Career

Robert & Beth,
So appreciate your friendship
over all these years.
Love you both,
"Everyone is in sales"

Chip

Chip Helm

Everyday Sales Wisdom for Your Life & Career
ISBN: 978-1-937514-79-2
By Chip Helm
© 2018 Chip Helm

Printed in the United States of America

Camden House Books LLC
Post Office Box 227
Broken Arrow, OK 74013
GetMyNewBook.com
Camden House Books, LKP-4479

Editorial Director: Dr. Larry Keefauver
Text Design/Layout: Lisa Simpson

Dedication

I have always used the K.I.S.S. method, "Keep it simple stupid" throughout my entire life. So why should I change now! Keep my dedication simple and sweet.

I truly with all my heart and soul want to dedicate my book to my beautiful, loving wife of twenty-six years, Cyrilla (Honey, I know that I married ten times up), and my three beautiful and smart children, Matthew, Michaela, and Sam.

I also dedicate my book to God who knew the kind of loving woman who would put up with me and be the mother of my children. I thank God every day of my life that He blessed me with a wonderful and loving family.

Acknowledgments

Two things inspired me to write this book. The first was my family. I have three beautiful children, Matthew, Michaela, and Sam. Matthew is the oldest and never wanted siblings. I bet that is not hard to believe from the oldest. He played tennis at Ball State. He is currently in medical school at Texas Tech. Michaela is my only daughter who has me wrapped around her pinky and is currently in vet school at Purdue. My youngest son, Sam plays football at Ball state and plans to go to Dental school.

I am the luckiest man on the planet to have a wife like Cyrilla, who has supported me through thick and thin. She has put up with me for twenty-six years. God really blessed by bringing her into my life.

About ten years ago, we were sitting around the fireplace over Christmas and talking about life in general.

I opened my big mouth and said, "I want to write a book about my experiences in sales."

I had always felt I had something to share and if I could impact one person, I win.

My three kids looked at me and said, "Write a book. That sounds like what you want to do."

I told them I was going to write a book and I wasn't going to wait until after I retired. I wanted to do it before I got out of sales. I wanted to share my thirty-two years of experiences while I was "in the heat of the moment." Everything I speak about I have been there, done it, and taken the test.

So, thank you to my family for pushing me to make this book a reality. I want to leave a legacy for my kids, and hopefully for all sales folks that come after me in the industry and my company.

I would remiss to not acknowledge one more person, and that is James "Butch" Rosser, one of the kindest and generous souls I have ever known. I know if it were not for "Butch," as his friends call him, I may not have ever started this journey of writing this book of life lessons.

As the story goes, I was talking to Butch one evening last June about my interest in pursuing my passion in writing this book; I didn't know how to get started, and I was scared to death.

He proceeded to listen to me go on and on about my fear until he stopped me right in the middle of my rambling and said, "I will help you get started." I said, "Okay!" Thank you Butch, I love you, man!

Table of Contents

Everyone Is in Sales

I don't think I would be interested in writing this book if I didn't think "Everyone is in Sales." All of us are in sales! It does not matter if you are in marketing, IT, Finance, HR, etc., you are in sales. You are either selling a widget, a concept, or more importantly yourself. If you are a hairdresser, a mechanic, or corporate CEO, you are in sales.

Sales is all about communicating; just imagine a conversation over a cup of coffee with a friend, building a trusting relationship, and putting their needs above yours. You should value and respect the other person's opinions, needs, and thoughts. You want to service others, treat them like you want to be treated. and if you put their needs first, then you will not try to take advantage of them, and therefore be nothing but honest, respectful, and fair to them. Remember you are selling every day of your life; most of the time you are trying to sell yourself, a service or a widget. By the way, communicating in sales or any relationship never seeks to:

- Dominate or control;

- Manipulate or use people;

- Intimate or create fear in others.

Sales most definitely embodies the ultimate value of the Golden Rule: *Do unto others as you would have them do unto you.*

WE LIVE BY THE
#GOLDENRULE
TREATING OTHERS LIKE WE WOULD LIKE TO BE TREATED.
IT HAS ALWAYS BEEN OUR GUIDING PRINCIPLE.

Sales is not rocket science; it does not have to be difficult. We make it more difficult than we need to make it. It doesn't have to be that challenging if you do the little things right. I use what's called the KISS method: "Keep It Simple Stupid." It is simply talking to customers, having fun, and finding out what they need. It is as simple as that.

If I had to think of two skills to perfect sales and communication, it would be repetition, repetition, repetition, and preparation, preparation, preparation! Just like you prepare and study a lot for an exam, you must prepare and prepare some more to have a successful conversation with every customer. Repetition is important because you need to practice your "spiel" (Scottish and Northern English) over and over and over so you can say it in your sleep. Sales is really repeating yourself over and over. I am still trying to perfect sales even after thirty-two years in the business.

I do not get bored because I am still learning and want to perfect my craft. No conversation I have with a customer is the same, but my "spiel" is because I must make sure I have my elevator speech (old school term for spiel) mastered before I talk to the customer. I have been working on my elevator speeches for years. I spend a lot of time in front of a mirror practicing. I drive other people batty when they look over and see me in the car talking to myself. I am just glad I don't answer myself; otherwise I would be in therapy (LOL). I believe talking out loud is one of the greatest and simplest ways to prepare and craft your two-minute elevator speech.

Do you know what to say in a couple of minutes? That is the million-dollar question that you must answer!

It takes a lot of repetition and preparation to become a great salesperson and the journey never ends. As you get better and better, what keeps you driven is the results. In sales, it is all about results. I'm not going to tell you that financial results don't impact you because they do. If your sales go up, that usually leads to bonuses, pay raises, etc.

However, what is even bigger than that in my mind is the relationships you derive through your conversations with customers. I am still in the business thirty-two years later because the relationships I have built are way beyond professional in nature. God gave me an ability to communicate, connect, and build long lasting relationships with people. I will share with you what I have learned over my thirty-two years of experience.

The truth is, no matter what road you choose and what career you end up in, you are in sales. Sales is part of what everyone does on a daily basis. For example, my son Matthew is in Medical School. He wants to become an Orthopedic Surgeon. He is in sales because once he has earned his degree, he has to draw customers to his office to see him and request his services. It doesn't matter what profession you are in. People tell me, "I'm in marketing, I'm in IT, I'm in supply chain," and they don't think they are in sales. I tell them, you are either selling a concept, you are selling a widget, or you are selling yourself.

My dad always used to say, "All medical professionals have the same GPA, the same test scores, and the same technical ability. What separates them from the best of the best is their **bedside manner.**" It's how they treat people. That is what sales is all about. Actually, it is what life is all about.

TREAT PEOPLE LIKE YOU WANT TO BE TREATED

AND YOU WILL BE REWARDED TEN-FOLD

WITH SUCCESSFUL CAREERS AND RELATIONSHIPS.

How do we simplify sales? Use the Kiss method: Keep It Simple Stupid. The bottom line is it is not supposed to be technical. Please keep it simple, don't overanalyze it, and don't over think it. If it doesn't become natural and you can't have fun talking to people, then think about a career change. Simplicity is what the "Kiss Method" is all about. KISS is an acronym used as a design principle by the U.S. Navy in 1960. The KISS principle states that most systems work best if they are kept simple rather than made complicated. Therefore, simplicity should be a key goal in design and unnecessary complexity should be avoided.

Here's the key for any career you choose. Whatever you end up doing in life has to become natural to you! Sometimes sales is made out to be too complex and it really isn't or it does not have to be. Sales is simply just you and the customer getting together, talking about a need they may have, and you building an honest and truthful relationship with them to solve that need. To help you do this, I will share with you my "Chipisms."

"CHIPISMS"

I came up with the term "Chipism" in a class one day while I was teaching at Ball State. I was in one of my excitable, passionate moods, and I kept feeling the students were mesmerized about some of my thoughts and comments.

Out of the blue, I yelled out to them, "I have a Chipism for you."

When I would say something important, something I wanted them to listen to, and something I wanted them to remember, I would say, "Chipism."

Chipisms became part of who I am, part of my DNA. Recently a student came up to me that I hadn't seen in two years, and the first thing he said was, "I remember some of your Chipisms."

To hear that is like music to my ears! So, I am going to give you some of my "Chipisms" starting here in Book 1. Good news, I have a second book, **Bigger Than Sales:** *How Humility and Relationships Build Career Success,* which will take your relationships, self-image, personal branding, and leadership/communication skills to the highest levels.

Chapter 1

Chip's Story

"You know what,
I do this for the love of the game,
not the money."
— **Cal Ripken**

I was born in Evansville, Indiana. My dad was an orthodontist. Mom was a very bright woman who had a stationary shop inside our house and she taught me everything I know about people skills. She had the ability to make people comfortable; consequently, they would often open up and tell her their life stories.

As the youngest sibling, I have four older sisters. So, you can just imagine that it probably didn't go well for me. It was tough having five women in the house. Dad and I were really outnumbered!

Growing up, I played three sports—basketball, football, and baseball. I didn't have much time to take on any job responsibilities. Between sports and school, there was no extra time to do manual labor type jobs. I could throw a football, hit a baseball, and shoot a basketball. I am very competitive and hate losing. Playing sports taught me a lot about competing and a lot about how to be a gracious loser. I ended up playing football briefly at Indiana University as a walk-on, which was even tougher back in those days. We weren't treated very well, but I enjoyed my experience. I think it also gave me a lot of insight in how to compete at a high level as I continued down my life's journey.

Choosing a Career Path

When I graduated from high school, my childhood dream was to be a dentist just like my dad. I wanted to have a wife, three kids, and live in a house with a white picket fence in Evansville, Indiana, working with my dad in his dental practice. My journey started as a little boy, continued in high school and college until I finally got accepted into dental school. During the third year of dental school, my career pursuit faltered; it became very apparent that I was struggling with waxing teeth and cutting tooth preps. I simply did not have the small hand-eye motor skills to continue in the dental field. I played sports growing up and didn't realize there is a difference between fine motor skills and the large hand-eye skills used for sports.

Realizing that dentistry was more about small hand and eye coordination, I felt like a failure because I could not master the skills needed. My only career path since childhood was now derailed; fear gripped me when I considered my future. I didn't have a Plan B, and I dreaded facing my father, telling him I was quitting dental school, and letting him down.

So, I wrote a letter to my father. On his birthday, which happened to be on Father's Day, June 15, 1985, we were all watching Dad open his gifts. I handed him my birthday card with a letter tucked inside. My heart was racing as I watched my father open the card, pull out the letter, and begin reading it. Suddenly, I begin to cry as I saw my dad tear up. I had never seen my dad cry before.

Dad commented that he never knew how much of a hardship it was on me in dental school! It was a tough, heartfelt moment for both of us. I had always wanted to be like dad and become a dentist. I never wanted to let my father down because in my mind, he walked on water.

We both remembered how years ago dad told me to go out and dig a one-foot hole in the ground. I don't even remember what the hole was for, but I dug for quite a while. Finally, I finished and rushed inside excitedly telling him I had finished the project.

He walked outside, looked down at the hole, and said, "Son, you have only dug a five-inch hole."

I just didn't have the depth perception or small motor skills to complete the job. Dad didn't realize until the day I told him I was leaving Dental School that the job digging the hole he'd asked me to do years earlier was a telltale sign that dentistry was not in my future.

WHEN A DREAM IMPLODES, WHAT DO YOU DO NEXT?

What's next when the thing you've been doing doesn't lead you into your next step in life? I had put all my efforts toward building a future into a dream that didn't fit my skills, interests, or giftings.

Dad asked me what my interests were, and we just began talking about what I thought I wanted to do when "I grow up." As we talked about dentistry, it became apparent that my focus wasn't on teeth; it was about the people I wanted to help. While working in the Dental Clinic, I had to have a professor next to me making sure I didn't make any mistakes. While my dental skills were lacking, my people skills always kept my dental chair full of people who wanted to see me. I had a steady stream of appointments all day long. Mothers with their daughters and sons loved to come to see me. They preferred to see me, but I knew it was not because I was a highly skilled dentist. So why were people lined up to see me? I realized God had given me the ability to communicate and connect with people.

Discover who you are.
Focus on the dream, gifts, and talents
God gave you.
Become who you are...
not what others want you to be.

When I left dental school shortly after my father's birthday, I headed to see Bill Armstrong, who was one of my mentor's. I had nowhere else to turn outside of my father to get some ideas on what was next in my life. I am very goal oriented, but my life's goal had suddenly changed and that was devastating.

"YOU WOULD BE GREAT IN SALES."

At this transition time in my life, the head of the Indiana University Foundation, Bill Armstrong, said to me, "Chip, I've got this great company I want you to work for. I think you would be great in sales."

Surprised, I asked, "Sales?"

My class schedule included nothing on business, finance, marketing, or sales. No one I knew had ever gone into sales. My focus had only been on a career in dentistry. Bill and I had met at the Little 500 Bike Race at Indiana University. At the race, I did what I always did—put my hand out to shake hands and introduce myself to anyone around me I didn't know. I have always enjoyed meeting people. Bill and I struck up a friendship from that first moment when I reached out to him; we remained great friends until his passing.

A communicator takes the initiative to reach out and connect with others.

So, when I went to him concerning my career dilemma, Bill told me he could get me an interview with Cook Medical. That is how my journey into sales began. Looking back, I believe that my experience in dental school opened my eyes to hard work, to fight through hardships in life, and showed me I had the ability to communicate and connect with people.

Lucky for me, Bill Armstrong believed in me and saw my potential in sales with my communicative skills and the way I connected with people. I trusted my mentor when he said this is a good fit for me. I went to that interview and was hired to work in sales for Cook Medical. It was a family-owned company, it stood by its family, its values, and they treated you like a person. They really cared about their customers and those who worked for them. It seemed like they just did the right things the right way. So, the first job I'd ever had was when I was twenty-five years old. I was on my way on my journey in sales.

Back then you didn't get much training. You pretty much just got out there, talked to customers, and really learned on the job. I ran around to hospitals, smiling and talking to people. What jazzed me about what I was doing was that I was selling something that impacted mankind. This medical company I went to work for treated very ill patients all over the world. I don't think I would have been very good in other type of sales.

I wanted to be like my father and help people. The Lord did provide me with an opportunity to use my communication skills and my love of people in this so-called profession of "sales." I had no idea what sales was all about, but I knew I could help people. I could sell something that impacted people's lives. I could do something that allowed people to live longer and people were benefiting from what I sold.

I fell in love with what I was doing in the first 6 months. I sold catheters. A catheter is a tube that is put in your body into veins and arteries. Through the catheters (tubes) you can infuse antibiotics, fluids, and even chemotherapeutic agents for cancer patients.

Communicating and connecting with people came naturally for me and I was just having fun. Though I had my hardships, I have always been like Cal Ripken. He is an old-time baseball player who played for the Baltimore Orioles. I remember watching baseball one day with my dad. Cal Ripken had just broken the record for playing the most games consecutively in baseball. One of the announcers said Cal Ripken had told him, "You know what, I do this for the love of the game, not the money." That is kind of like me, I do it for the love of what we do. I love what we do for patients and not for the money.

I SAY I ALWAYS SELL FOR THE LOVE OF SAVING PEOPLE'S LIVES.

I think it begins and ends with my difficult journey through dental school. Dental school showed me what I couldn't do very well, but it also opened my eyes up to what I can do very well. I found out that people embraced me or connected to me or they found something about me that they liked. I would not be where I am today if it wasn't for my experiences in the Dental Clinic many years ago. I learned that people gravitated to me. Maybe they liked my honesty and my transparency was refreshing for the parents of the patients I served in the Dental Clinic. Serving others with a smile on my face and kindness in my heart is part of who I am. It is a part of my desire to help others. I always use the phrase, "service others." If you service others, I promise you will get tenfold back.

IT IS ALL ABOUT PEOPLE, WHAT CAN I DO TO SERVICE THEM, AND MAKE THEM SUCCESSFUL.

It was God's plan for me to go through dental school to learn about successes, failures, and servicing others. I still wake up every day and think about the impact of all the patients in the world that I have helped and that what we sell does make a difference. I still can't believe they pay me to communicate and work with people.

I HAVE BEEN LIVING A DREAM FOR THIRTY-TWO YEARS.

"Chipisms"

At the end of each chapter, I will offer you insights on what I have learned over my thirty-two years in "sales." Take a few moments and see how what I have learned impacts where you are in your career journey.

❧ Communicating and connecting with people came naturally for me.

> *What comes easy for you?*

❧ I fell in love with what I was doing in the first 6 months.

> *Are you in love with what you are now doing?*

❧ Lucky for me, Bill Armstrong believed in me and saw my potential in sales with my communicative skills and the way I connected with people.

> *Do you have someone like Bill Armstrong in your life?*

❧ It was God's plan for me to go through dental school to learn about successes, failures, and servicing others.

> *Can you see God's plan for your life and career through the things you have experienced in life?*

> *What have you learned through these experiences that will now help you move forward with the right career path for your life?*

I HAVE BEEN LIVING A DREAM FOR THIRTY-TWO YEARS. SO CAN YOU!

Chapter 2

Never Had a Job in My Life

"If you love what you do, you'll never
work another day in your life."
— Mark Twain

MY SECRET SAUCE

If you were to ask me, "What's the secret to your success in sales?" I would probably answer, "What you see is what you get. I am honest as the day is long. I will tell you like it is, even if you don't want to hear it or like what I have to say." I do believe honesty is the best policy. I also have discovered, sometimes people don't share what really is going on. They want to sugar coat things, but I do not do that to people. I share the good, the bad, and the ugly.

Over the last thirty-two years, I have often wished that my mentors would have given me some guidance on what to be careful of, what to watch out for, and how to be more self-aware in some situations. Maybe I would have made fewer mistakes and gone down a better path. Perhaps I would have become the CEO of our company.

I don't know, but it would have been interesting to see what may have happened if one of my mentors would have shared a few more secrets to success when I was younger.

However, having traveled this journey has lead me to share with you the successes and the heartaches I have experienced. Please understand that I will share in a way that is at times raw, so heartfelt, real, honest, and with such passion that you know I am earnestly seeking to connect with you. Please take seriously what I am telling you. I wouldn't lead you down the wrong path, especially since I have made some wrong decisions and I desire to help you avoid the same mistakes I have made.

I always say that sales is not rocket science, but I have felt like I have been on a bit of a rocket ship for the last thirty-two years. I have had my ups and downs and have been knocked down a lot. I plan to transparently share the bitter and the sweet to this journey hoping to better equip you for yours.

Never Had a Job in My Life

Many people don't even have one passion in life, but I have three: my family, the company I work for, and our home in northern Michigan. I have had these three passions most of my life. You can see why it is easy for me to get up every day and go into work! That is the key. I go into work every day with a big smile on my face. I like what the President of Sony said in an article I read a long time ago. He was asked what he did for enjoyment outside of work. He responded by saying other than spending time with his family, he loved to work. I am the same way. Outside of my family, I love talking to customers and taking care of people. It is not considered work to me to talk to customers on the weekend and make sure we take care of their needs.

I have been on the sixteenth hole, enjoying a round of golf, and a customer calls with an urgent request or even a simple question, and I will answer the phone and hear what they need. Then I will go back to hitting the golf ball and feel good about helping that person.

THE PROCESS

Step 1: You must enjoy the art of communication and building relationships with people. That is what sales is all about. Everyone is in sales. We either sell widgets or a concept, but more importantly we sell ourselves. Now, I do not have the time and space here to develop the full scope of the importance of good communication. In my next book, **Bigger Than Sales:** *How Humility and Relationships Build Career Success*, I devote an entire chapter to how to communicate effectively.

Step 2: Figure out what kind of sales you want to go into. A bestselling author and friend who is also a counselor, consultant, and minister quips, "Everyone is selling something—a product, a service, a message, or a person including himself or herself." If you like selling, then it is like a building block. You build on that and then you start doing it every day and you will have successes. Make a difference. Have a passion to impact others positively. When you do, it jazzes you to get up every morning

Step 3: Enjoy it. This is where it gets into your blood and you are having fun. Once you have one win and it turns into a second and third win, you start to like it more and maybe even love it. I believe you will find your passion faster and quicker if you do not focus on the almighty dollar, though. Too many people come out and look at the dollar and then the passion doesn't follow. If you don't treat your work like it's all about the money, then you will find your passion first. If you love something and you work hard, the money comes. If you strive just for the money, you probably won't like what you are doing.

Money does not drive passion,
but passion does drive money!

Step 4: Cultivate a great work ethic and discipline. Find that right company or start that right business that has values which align with yours. I am still at my current company after thirty-two years because they are family and they have family values that align with what I want in a family and a company. I like the way they treat us. We are not a number; each person in the company is treated and respected as a unique, gifted human being. Anyone in the company can talk to the president or any of the executives. It is all about people.

You must enjoy the people that you work with. That is how you fall in love with any company. The values and the philosophy a company have are what drives everyone working there to become very passionate about what he or she does.

I am more passionate today than I was thirty-two years ago. I feel like I have as much or even more energy today than I did ten years ago. Why? Because I love what I do. I have seen the results. I see patients who have been served by what we do. I have worked with colleagues who are performing well and doing well. I have been blessed to be in leadership roles with opportunities to coach and mentor people. That continues to invigorate and drive me because I am seeing results and the fruit of my labor.

Relationship building at work is like a good marriage. It is not the same thing, but it is the same kind of feeling you have when you get up every morning and you have a smile on your face and you want to go to work. You get to that point and you know that it is a good thing. You must have that kind of passion and love for what you do, or you will not be successful.

**You can be passionate about your work
just like you are passionate for your spouse.**

I have such a passion and love for what I do, I am always smiling about it and I always have good things to say about it. I am a zealot about how we can help patients. I love it so much I am amazed they pay me to do this. It just seems very simple to me, natural, and what I really want to do. That's why I say I've never had a job in my thirty-two years.

This is the kind of passion I have had for a long time. It is that sustained passion and perseverance that has driven me to be successful. I feel like I have been on a long journey and fortunate to find what I love to do. There was a leadership conference I attended and heard some powerful leaders from around the country. Angelo Duckworth, from the Global Leadership Summit in August 2017, said, "Grit = Sustained Passion + Perseverance for a long time." I have had a sustained passion for thirty-two years. I have just persevered through everything along the way on this journey. So, I guess you could say I have had a lot of "grit," too.

A great friend of mine, James "Butch" Rosser, a prominent surgeon, said the following about me, "Just in reviewing this book, I know that taking care of people has been a high priority as to what makes you tick. The other thing was competition through your activity and sports; you thrive in competition. So, as I now sit back and look at it, you know you took not being able to finish school, you took one step back to take a leap forward to what you are today because your thing, your why, your why you live, why you breathe—you found it in sales. Sales tapped into your competition, but then being with that company that produced products that touched people's lives in a healing way, that hit your heart and your core."

SHARE AND MENTOR

I also feel like I have been called by God to work with people, share my life lessons, and mentor young adults. My son, Matthew decided to go to Ball State to continue his studies after High School and play Division 1 tennis. When I drove Matthew up to Ball State the summer before school started, I asked where the Sales and Marketing Departments were located. I walked over there to find out more about what they were doing to teach their students about potential sales careers. Lo and behold, I ran right into the head of the Sales and Marketing Dept, Ramon Avila. I introduced myself and said I would like to share with students my experiences in sales and was there any opportunity to come in and speak to his students.

One thing led to another and five years later, I have now gone across the state of Indiana to Ball State, the Kelly School of Business at IU, Butler, Indiana State, and Purdue University to share not only my successes, but more importantly where I have failed. I don't know if you would call it "pearls of wisdom" or "tricks and tips." I would just say I share the Good, the Bad, and the Ugly of my sales journey over the past thirty-two plus years. I encourage you to find ways to share with others what you have learned in your journey—pass it on!

"CHIPISMS"

❧ I believe most people don't even have one passion in life and I have three.

What have you discovered is your passion?

❧ **Step 1:** You must enjoy the art of communication and building relationships with people.

Does this describe you?

Why is this an important first step if you are going into sales?

❧ **Step 2:** Figure out what kind of sales you want to go into.

Have you completed this step yet?

Why is it so important to your success in sales?

❧ **Step 3:** Is where it gets into your blood and you are having fun.

Are you having fun at what you're currently doing the majority of the time?

Why or why not?

❧ **Step 4:** You also must have a great work ethic.

How would others describe your work ethic?

Have you discovered things you need to change in this area?

❧ Did you know you could have the same passion/love for your career as you do for your spouse?

33

✤ I have such a passion and love for what I do, I am always smiling about it and I always have good things to say about it.

How do you talk about what you are currently doing?

✤ I have persevered through everything along the way on this journey. So, I guess you could say I have had a lot of "grit," too.

Do you have "grit" when it comes to persevering through trials at what you are currently doing?

✤ I also feel like I have been called by God to work with people, share my life lessons, and mentor young adults.

Has God called you to share with others what you have learned along your personal journey?

Why not begin keeping a journal so when the time comes, you can share what you have learned with the next generation?

Chapter 3

"Chipisms" about Character

"Be more concerned with your character than your reputation,
because your character is what you really are,
while your reputation is merely what others think you are."
— **John Wooden**[1]

"Do the Right Thing"

Kem Hawkins, Ex-CEO of Cook Medical, taught me the golden rule of, "Do the right thing" and in the medical language, "Do right by the patient." Every day, look yourself in the mirror and ask the question, "Am I doing the right thing"? Always be ethical and have the highest integrity. If you do it with the right intent and the right heart, I believe you will do the right thing. When you go to sleep at night, you need to be comfortable with yourself.

I always say two things when I lay my head on the pillow each night, "Did I do everything I could for my company and did I not screw anyone over or throw them under the bus today?"

---

[1] https://www.brainyquote.com/quotes/john_wooden_163015?src=t_character

You are the only person who can answer both those questions. If you keep in mind you are going to have to answer these questions every night, you will think twice before doing anything that might damage your integrity and your relationship with your company and your customers.

In the thirty-two years I have worked in this profession, I never intentionally hurt anyone. Many people feel sales is a cut-throat business, but it does not have to be that way. I just don't believe that is the way to get ahead in any career.

Sales should be built on relationships
that reflect your integrity and good work ethics.

"Johnny on the Spot"

I am always there for customers, friends, and family. Basically, people I have a relationship with know that if they need anything, I will be there for them. This is actually a Chipism within a Chipism because another part of being called "Johnny on the Spot" is:

Follow up + Follow through = Success

You have got to be there all the time and all in as well as be willing to put yourself out there taking risks to take good care of your relationships to be successful at any career, but especially in sales. Unfortunately, I think "Johnny on the Spot" is not what we typically see across any industry.

Another facet of being "Johnny on the Spot" is, "Do what you say you are going to do and do it when you say you are going to do it." If you live by that every day, you will be very successful. For example, if I made a promise I would be at your office at 9:00 a.m., I would be there by 8:30 a.m. waiting for you.

Here is a rule to live by: Never use traffic or the alarm didn't go off as excuses not to be on time for a meeting or an appointment! Just get up earlier and leave earlier so you will be there early even if you encounter delays beyond your control. Excuses hold no credence with customers, bosses, or other important relationships.

"To be on Time is to be Early" needs to be a behavior that becomes part of who you are both personally and professionally. If you want to move up the corporate ladder and receive nice raises, show up at all meetings early. More importantly, show up early to meet with your customers! You never know when their schedule may have changed, and by showing up early, you can still connect with them.

Being on time is being early or being on time is not being late. You could look at it either way. If there is a 9 o'clock meeting, you ought to be there at 8:45 at the latest. I really believe that you must do this both in your professional and your personal life.

**Being on time shows others their time
is more valuable to you than yours!**

When a secretary of George Washington excused himself for being late by saying that his watch was too slow, the reply of Washington was, "You must get a new watch, or I must get a new secretary."[2]

---

[2] http://www.specialty-calendars.com/punctuality.html

"Honest as the Day Is Long"

If someone is "honest as the day is long," they are very honest. They are a consistent, reliable person. The implication seems to be that he or she is honest all the time, twenty-four hours a day, not just when someone is looking. I am going to tell you emphatically, honesty is always the best policy. I personally wear everything on my sleeve, so to speak. What you see is what you get with me.

However, that does not mean that your honesty won't be interpreted incorrectly. Sometimes when you are too open with people because you have such a comfort level with them, it might come off as TMI (Too Much Information). Nevertheless, stay strong, never change, and always be honest. You can sleep much better at night if you are honest 24 hours a day!

A boyhood friend of mine, Mark Grobbel, knew I was going through some trying times with my siblings over our family home in Northern Michigan. We have been boyhood friends since we were five years old. We agree to disagree most of the time, so what he proceeded to tell me one day when he called me was surprising.

"Chip, you are so honest that if God came down to Earth and told you it was okay to lie, you still would not lie! You are the type that would have gone ahead and done it the right way, I mean that is how honest you are. I have never known anybody as honest as you. Even if you had done something wrong, you would show it on your face. 'I messed up' would have been plastered all over your forehead because that is just who you are."

I guess that says it all about who I am and how important it is to be as honest as the day is long.

Honesty is absolutely the best policy when you are working with your customers. Customers will appreciate your honesty and transparency with them. It is important that if you are having a conversation and the customer asks you something, you are honest with your responses. If you don't know something, just tell the client that you don't know, and you will get back as soon as possible with the answers. There is nothing wrong with not having all the answers for your customer. They actually will hold you in the highest regard when you don't try to dance around their question and you're just honest when you say, "I don't know."

"I don't know" is probably the best response you can have in any sales career unless you are totally sure about your information. Don't take a chance hurting your relationship with a customer by not being completely honest with them. It doesn't mean you are not credible, it doesn't mean you are not knowledgeable, it doesn't mean you are not a good salesperson when you tell them directly, "I don't know." You have raised the bar with the customer when you are completely honest. However, make sure you keep the second part of your honesty and get them the answer they need as soon as possible. Do what you say you will do when you say you will do it.

Do what you say you are going to do, and do it when you say you are going to do it!

This is a very simple, but very powerful life concept. If you promise something to the customer, follow up and fulfill the promise. If you don't make good on your promise, you will lose the customer and lose the business. That is a fact! In fact, you could lose out on a lot of personal relationships in life if you do not follow this essential concept.

"It's All About People"

I would not be here today if it wasn't for the people I serve: customers, reps, colleagues, and friends. The people I have worked with over the years have impacted me personally as well as professionally. Many of my customers have developed into friendships and many of my colleagues are now close friends of mine. The people you work with and serve every day are "what makes the world go round." That is why people stay with our company. When your work ethic includes the mindset that it is all about the people you work with and the customers you serve, you earn your customer's business and build mutually beneficial relationships. That leads into my next "Chipism."

"Customers Buy from People They Like"

Here is a quote from a wise friend of mine: "People do not buy from salespeople because they understand their products; they buy because they felt the salesperson understood their problems." People buy when the pain and the problem is greater than the cost of the solution. It goes back to the relationship you have with the customer. If the customers like you and you have a good product that is as good or better than competition, the customer will buy the product from you. Therefore, part of your responsibility to your customer is to be a problem solver.

"Be a Problem Solver"

Customers never forget you if you solve their problem. A problem solver will literally have the customer "in their pocket" and they will be loyal "until the cows come home." To become an effective problem solver, you need to have good listening skills. I am an effective communicator because I know when to talk and when to listen. Presenting the benefits of your product is ineffective if you do not know your customer's needs. They don't care about all the things your product will do unless you can show them how it will solve their specific problem. Unfortunately, many times we are so enthusiastic about presenting the wonders of our product, we neglect to first determine what the customer really needs and wants.

Listening = Hearing + Understanding
(their problem)

"TREAT PEOPLE LIKE YOU WANT TO BE TREATED"

I think this is the number one, golden rule in business, and basically the way you want to work with or lead people. You think it's something everyone does every day, but in all honesty, we need more people living by that credence. Try looking for three people daily to thank or tell them how much their friendship means to you, or just do a good deed for them. Wouldn't this world be a better place if we all just positively impacted three lives every day?

"Life is a series of experiences, each one of which makes us bigger, even though sometimes it is hard to realize this. For the world was built to develop character, and we must learn that the setbacks and grieves which we endure help us in our marching onward." — Henry Ford[3]

---

[3] https://www.brainyquote.com/quotes/henry_ford_151860?src=t_character

"Chipisms"

"Business Is Always Personal"

Business must become "Personal" for you to have long term success. How do these Character Chipisms lead to successful personal and business relationships?

- They build a trusting, loyal relationship.

- They bring in personal connections that align with the customer.

- They inspire you to take care of your customer!

Use the following as a checklist and see where you may need improvement in your character development.

☐ "Do the Right Thing."

☐ "Johnny on the Spot."

☐ "Honest as the Day Is Long."

☐ "It's All About People."

☐ "Customers Buy from People They Like."

☐ "Be a Problem Solver."

☐ "Treat People Like You Want to Be Treated."

☐ "Do what you say you are going to do, when you say you are going to do it!"

Now come up with a way to improve your weak areas. You will be very glad you did!

The Buck Stops Here

"Man must cease attributing his problems
to his environment and learn to exercise his will—
his personal responsibility in the realm of faith and morals."
—Albert Schweitzer[4]

Look yourself in the mirror. "If you are having a great year in your sales territory, it is you who did it. Pat yourself on the back. If you are not having a good year in sales, it is you who did it." Take complete ownership of your performance; good or bad. If you never make excuses and blame others when you are having a tough year, you will be very successful.

The difference between an average salesperson and a great salesperson is the great sales person never complains or makes excuses even when they had a bad day or month. The average salesperson seems to always make excuses about a bad day or month.

"The Buck Stops Here" is an expression I use often to say, "No Excuses, No Excuses, No Excuses." If you begin your career with the mindset that you take complete ownership for everything and make "no excuses," it will lead you to success in sales.

---

[4] http://www.azquotes.com/author/13192-Albert_Schweitzer/tag/responsibility

How do you learn how to take complete ownership and make no excuses?

You have to be really honest and transparent with yourself. You must look at yourself in the mirror and really reflect on yourself and be true to yourself.

If you have done a great job in your sales territory and you are selling a lot, it is because of you. If you are not selling a lot and you are not doing very well, it's because of you. Don't fall into the trap of complaining about and blaming the product, the data sheet, and the marketing tools for why you're not successful.

Success is
your own personal responsibility.

I have many examples in which a rep did not take personal responsibility for failure. One is a rep who said he didn't make it to the appointment to see the customer because of traffic. Then another time, he didn't make it to see the customer because his alarm clock didn't go off. Truthfully, we all have control of both these situations because we choose to get up early and leave early. Don't leave anything to chance when it concerns the needs of a customer. Those are just terrible excuses that will not sit well with any customer or boss.

Other typical excuses with many people include, "I don't have the videotape, the right marketing tools, or the right widget to sell." One salesperson told me he was waiting for "the next generation," the newer and improved widget. He added, "I will sell more of the widgets when the newer device comes out." However, if we were to look closely at their sale numbers, we would see they never sold the first-generation device very well. Reps are always looking for "bigger and better" widgets to sell are usually not selling what is in their bag already.

When the sales person feels like the buck doesn't stop with them, it will have impactful ramifications for them. One obvious result is they are not selling very much and not meeting sales goals. Therefore, they will most likely not be one of the company's top salespeople.

Another ramification is you may get to the point in your career where you are not going to get promoted because you are always making excuses, always complaining, and always blaming others for your outcome and your poor performance. In today's world, one of the major causes for lack of promotion is not taking personal responsibility for poor sales performance. Great salespeople never make excuses for what is happening in their territory, their performance, or why they didn't get the job done!

Peer and Customer Credibility

You are not going to be perceived as a hardworking, team player by your colleagues if you are making excuses and blaming others for your lack of sales. They are going to see it and hear it at meetings. Your colleagues will also see your poor sales results and you are not going to have their respect. You are not going to have that creditability among your peers. I think peer credibility is huge. Everyone wants to be perceived by their boss and peers as credible, honest, and true to their word.

Not taking personal responsibility can kill a relationship with a customer as well. It may not be directly connected to dishonesty, but it is perceived by the customer that you may not be completely honest with them because you are making excuses. For example, you couldn't get them a certain widget, or information, or a video and you make it look like it is the company's fault not yours. You end up hurting both the company's and your reputation with the customer.

Don't con yourself, customers can see right through you. So, just own up and remember you represent your company. Don't make it out to be your company's fault. If anything, put the blame on yourself. The customer will hold you in high esteem if you just admit you made a mistake. You do not want to lose your trust factor with the customer.

Sometimes when you are trying to go up the corporate ladder, you run head on into situations where company executives think you did something wrong even when you and everyone else do not think you did anything wrong. This is where the buck has to stop with you because it would be so easy to cry, get down, and blame someone else. You might be in someone's dog house for a while, but the best course of action is move forward. Take ownership for whatever you are told you did and work on not getting yourself in that situation again.

I coach people to watch your environment, watch what you say, use your ears, and don't bring alcohol into a business situation. A good example is if you are at company sales meeting, be cognizant of who is at the table with you and who is at the bar with you. Watch your words and what you drink. You will be very glad you take these precautions.

Here are some tips to get through this type of unfortunate situation:

- Be patient and just take it in stride.

- Get back up and dust yourself off.

- Don't get mad. You can't have vengeance.

- Accept it, move on, and try to forget about it.

- Control what you can control.

- Be the best you can at work in your current position. Actions speak louder than words. If you are doing really well at work, it will eventually prove itself out.

- Continue to be yourself and always do things with the right intent and right heart.

Dig deep, take ownership, admit wrong doing, and move on knowing you conquered "The Buck Stops Here!"

THE LITTLE 500

"The Little 500" is a bike race that is put on at Indiana University every spring. It is a race that is modeled after the Indianapolis 500 and was featured in a movie years ago called, "Breaking Away." There are four riders on each team using just one bike in a relay type bike race. There is an exchange of the bike with the next rider. Each team has three attempts to qualify. Each of the four riders must ride one complete lap to qualify for the race.

It was my senior year and we had yet to qualify for the race. I was the last rider and this was our last attempt to qualify. I was either going to mess up or qualify the team. It had come down to this third attempt and this last lap.

It was cold, rainy, and dark outside. I had not touched the bike in the first two qualifications because it didn't even get to me before we messed up. You mess up when you either fall off the pedals of the bike, or during the exchange the next rider falls off the pedals, or you don't get the bike to the next person appropriately. I had to take the bike from my teammate and get on the bike cleanly. There would be no excuses. I would be to blame if I fell and didn't finish my lap.

I can still see it today. I can still visualize the bike coming toward me as I said to myself, *It's up to me. There are going to be no excuses because if I don't get on this bike right and do this right, we lose.* I took responsibility right then and there.

Fortunately, I did get on the bike and we did qualify, but it was always in my mind that if I didn't qualify and if I didn't do it, there would be no excuses. I wasn't going to blame anybody else. I didn't blame my teammates when they messed up in the first two rounds, either. You never blame others!

Honesty Is at the Core

I look at honesty as the core of not making excuses and taking complete ownership and responsibility with everything you do. It must be an honesty that lies within you. If you are not honest to the bone, you won't be honest with your peers, your customers, and yourself. If you are not being truly honest with yourself, you will blame others for your misgivings and you won't be very successful.

I believe I read somewhere of a study that said only 25 percent of all sales people across all industries take full ownership if they do not perform well. This 25 percent believe they control their successes and they are absolutely right. I believe we have a moral and ethical responsibility to be "Honest as the day is long." Therefore, we must do things with the right integrity, the right moral values, and the right heart.

I believe we should be honest at all costs
and always take personal responsibility
for our actions.

I think "The Buck Stops Here" (meaning taking *personal responsibility*) is one of the greatest skills that can lead you to success in sales. Unfortunately, most people aren't good at learning this skill. They think other people control their successes or their failures, but that's not true. This is something people must embrace and understand early in their sales career to truly move forward with success from day one.

However, whether you are new to sales or have been doing it for a while, here are five things you can do to ensure that the buck stops with you:

- Be honest with yourself and stay true to yourself.

- Always take ownership and don't blame others.

- Start early in life looking yourself in mirror and reflect practicing when something happens to you.

- Even if you think you may be right, take ownership, and responsibility anyway.

- When you make mistakes, admit them before someone else confronts you. Don't hesitate to say you are sorry.

EXAMINE YOUR EXCUSES

In order to really take responsibility for your actions, you need to deal with the issue of excuses. Start by just admitting you make excuses. It is like a person that goes to AA, you go to EE (Excuses, Excuses), you just stand up and say I make excuses. Most people make excuses and they usually don't even realize they are doing it.

A good way to do this is to make a list of the excuses you make, consider why you make them, and decide which ones you want to work on stopping. Perhaps keep a journal on when and where you did not take personal responsibility and used excuses. This will help you become more aware of even your "unconscious" use of excuses.

Face the Facts: As with most bad habits, the first step is to acknowledge you have this problem. Don't procrastinate and hope it will resolve itself.

Get Over Yourself: Because you have never acknowledged your own responsibility in making excuses, maybe you have felt like people are out to get you. Well, it's time to leave the conspiracy theories to Oliver Stone and stop being paranoid. There will always be people who disagree with you, criticize you unjustly, or disrespect you. Don't play the blame game. Instead of focusing on what others are doing to you (that's paranoia), learn from your mistakes and improve.

Clarify Expectations: If you restrict yourself to tasks that you can realistically accomplish, you won't be tempted to make excuses for your failings. Set realistic, pragmatic goals. Be upfront when asked to plan the office team-building activity. Ask what time commitment is required before you take it on. Don't feel forced to accept if you know that you'll end up laying the blame on others when you fall short.

Stop Complaining: Constant hypercriticism of others doesn't make you look any better. Stop shirking responsibility and looking for the easy way out. Remind yourself each day of the negative implications of constantly finding excuses. Drive yourself to change.

Speak up, then Shut up: Learn to say you're sorry without launching into a long-winded explanation. The reasons your report was late doesn't matter. If you forgot your wedding <u>anniversary</u>, face the music and apologize without hiding behind fictitious reasons. Challenge yourself to eliminate extraneous excuses starting right now.

Accept Criticism: Take ownership of your shortcomings and mistakes, but don't let habitual faultfinders undermine your confidence. You may be reinventing your attitude, but not everyone else is, so don't let others force you to revert to your old defensive ways. When you receive criticism, ask for specifics. In your annual performance review, discuss ways to improve for the future rather than trying to rewrite the past.

Develop a Buddy System: Make a pact with a friend or colleague who has the same problem. Agree to point it out if you see him regressing to his old ways and have him commit to doing the same for you.

There's No Excuse

Your health and well-being are your own responsibility. You have choices in life, and you're entitled to choose to find excuses for yourself, to blame other people, and to sound paranoid. However, you'll be happier and healthier if you opt for honesty, integrity, and confidence.

"Chipisms"

How you react to external events is one of the things that will form people's impressions of you. It's never too late to improve your image. Show your willingness to change by creating solutions instead of excuses. It takes time and effort to change, but it will be worth it.

> Accept the reality of your situation and don't blame others.

> Understand that it is not going to change overnight, so be patient with yourself.

> *Move on with honesty, the right intent, and the right heart.*

> Concentrate on your work and what you can control and let what you can't control roll off your back.

> Use self-analysis so you really understand what is going on with your performance.

> Be careful with your words, speak less, and listen more. Observe your environment and be more self-aware.

Chapter 5

Less Is More

"You are what you repeatedly do.
Excellence is not an event - it is a habit."
— **Aristotle**[5]

Due to their inexperience, many new salespeople will "throw up" on customers. They want to interject too much information when they are in a meeting. That is why I say that "less is more." You don't have to know a lot of information in sales. You just need to know the **right information** to sell to the customer you have the appointment with that day. What I am saying is simply "know enough" to sell the widget, the concept or yourself. Sometimes, we can be over trained or informed and have too much information beyond what the customer or client needs. It's nice to know all that stuff, but that won't sell it to the customer.

For example, when you prepare for a meeting, especially with a new customer, you want to know the company and the type of widget that you want to sell them. I'd much rather you know a few facts about the company and widget really well, instead of trying to know everything, and then you get your facts and information all confused when you are face-to-face with your customer.

---

5 http://www.intenseexperiences.com/motivational-sales-quotes.html

What I have observed over the years is people try to learn too much about a widget, and they end up not being very good at anything else. They walk into the customer's office, don't listen as well as they should, and "throw up" on the customer. They have so much information upstairs in their head, they just start rambling. They think they will impress the customer with all their knowledge, but downloading too much information all at once can often cause a destructive overload. They would have been better off spending their time preparing a couple of things to tell the customer. When they know their information well, they can convey it in an intelligent way versus just rambling on and not really having a good understanding of anything at all.

Learn a few things really well.
I guarantee you will be very successful in sales.

How Do You Learn a Few Things Well?

If I had to think of two skills to perfect sales, I would say to you, "Repetition and Preparation!" If you were studying for an important exam, you would prepare and study a lot. Well, it is the same for your meetings with every customer. You have to prepare and prepare some more then you can have a successful conversation! Repetition is just as important because you need to practice your sale's "spiel" over, and over, and over so you can say it in your sleep. Sales is really repeating yourself again and again.

I speak a lot about "Repetition and Preparation" because getting great in sales is a long process. I am still trying to perfect sales even after thirty-two years in the business. I do not get bored because I am still learning. That's because no conversation I have with a customer is the same, even though my "spiel" is. I have made sure I have my elevator speech mastered so I can present it confidently and smoothly in front of the customer.

I have been working on my "elevator speeches" for years. I spend a lot of time in front of a mirror practicing and talking to myself. I believe talking out loud is one of the greatest and simplest ways to prepare and craft your elevator speech. The key is less is more. You need to perfect your "2-minute elevator speech."

"Most salespeople talk way too much," says Entrepreneur Magazine. "In today's market, chatty salespeople are chomping at the bit to overwhelm prospects with information. Research shows that the average salesperson talks over 81 percent of the time in a selling situation. Not only is that approach ineffective, it's losing you <u>sales</u>. You can close more sales, simply by talking less. A great salesperson will talk no more than 20 percent of the time in a selling situation. Close your mouth a little more and you might just find you'll close many more deals as a result."[6]

Do you know what to say in a couple of minutes?

That is the million-dollar question that you should be able to answer! It takes a lot of *Repetition and Preparation* to become a great salesperson and the journey never ends. I think most people get that Preparation is important to any successful career, but understanding the importance of Repetition is another story. Not only do we need to use a repetitive skill to learn our spiel, but also the best way for

[6] https://www.entrepreneur.com/article/229577 - "The Secret to Closing More Sales: Talk Less."

salespeople to learn what they are being taught is to say it over and over and over again. So much of what we say from day to day is repetitive in nature, but it needs to be delivered in a very natural way. Now you may ask…

- *How do you get your spiel to the point where it becomes natural and you can actually do it in your sleep?*

- *How do you perfect your "two-minute elevator speech"?*

You need to prepare your repetition of the same conversations about the same project every day. You may have some tweaks about it for a specific situation or customer, but it pretty much comes out the same way every time you say it. You have got to repeat and repeat it until it comes out like as what I call, "Natural Memorization." You have memorized it, but your delivery is so smooth because you know it so well, it does not sound memorized to the customer.

You are only as good at repeating it if you understand it. Understanding it is just as important as being able to repeat it to yourself and to the customer. However, if you don't know what you are talking about, the memorized mumble jumble won't come off the tongue with confidence and believability.

BECOMING THE KING OF PREPARATION

One trick in becoming the king of preparation that I still do. I am driving down the road on my way to a sales call, I am talking out loud to myself. I go through step one, step two, step three of what am I going to talk about. Then I go through my checklist: What are my objectives and goals? Do I have the right materials? Do I have my business card to leave behind after the sales call?

Another tip to continue your preparation is to review these "5 Truths of Sales:"

1. **Follow-up + Follow Through = Success**. Quickly get back to your customers and do what you say you are going to do, when you say you are going to do it.

2. **Network**. You must learn the art of networking to build your customer base. Get out of your comfort zone and put your hand out to meet people. In my second book, **Bigger Than Sales:** *How Humility and Relationships Build Career Success,* I share the importance of networking and how to have the right people in it.

3. **Build Positive Relationships.** Relationship building is a unique skill you need to develop. Figure out how to relate to people and build the right connections with people and you will build a relationship that is long term, not short term.

4. **Cultivate a Good Attitude.** Everything is about attitude and having a positive attitude. How do you react to an unexpected situation? Success breeds success. Negativity breeds negativity. 75-80 percent of your attitude is how you react to a situation. Zig Ziglar's famous quote is, "Your attitude, not your aptitude, will determine your altitude."

5. **Be Passionate about your work, products, and services.** Passion is what it is all about. Find your passion and you will not let yourself fail.

READING YOUR CUSTOMER

Here is what really can go sideways in a sales call. You meet with indifferent customers or one that you sense does not like you. You do not want anything to do with them, but that does not matter. You need to figure them out and put your personal feelings aside. The customer is always right, so it does not matter if they do not click with you. It does not matter if they do not have a very good personality. They are your assignment for that appointment.

You must learn to read each of your customers; remember that non-verbal communication is 90 percent of what's being communicated. We must figure them out. They do not have to figure us out. Why I say this is because I have observed this with many companies and people across the industry. If the salesperson does not click with someone or if they do not like someone because of their personality, they do not believe they can develop them as a customer.

I have seen a colleague of mine not like a specific customer that I liked. Does this sound familiar to you? And it went south fast for both me and the customer; especially when my colleague had influence over working with this customer and could stop projects with the customer. So, when you have a customer you can work with that another person in your company cannot get along with, what should we feel and do?

The responsibility for learning how to work with and keep a customer is on us; the customer should not have to figure us out; we need to adapt to the needs of the customer. So, my colleague who didn't like working with that customer put me in an awkward position because I could not convince my colleague that the customer was right. My colleague had a personality conflict with the customer and could not adapt or change. The moral of this story is *put your own bias away and take care of the customer.* My Chipism here is, "I never met a customer I did not like." I hope you get my point!

Sales is all about Preparation and Repetition.

All throughout the book, you will read about "Preparation and Repetition." In sales, you can't prepare enough when learning and when having conversations with customers. You are only as good as your preparation. It is as simple as that!

One of legendary basketball coaches, John Wooden's famous quotes is, "Failing to prepare is preparing to fail."

Salespeople learn faster when messages are repeated over and over. The more things are repeated, the more likely you will put it to memory, and you will be able to say it to customers without even thinking about it.

I use repetitive learning when I do presentations. I repeat my messages to myself until "I am blue in the face." I still rehearse and go over any content many times before I go into any meeting with customers. When I teach sales courses to our sales folks, I get in the habit of repeating the same messages again and again throughout the course. You may feel like I have repeated this message again and again in this chapter. The truth is, I have. Do you get it?

Repetition is key to learning because most of the skills we need are behavioral in nature.

"PLAN YOUR WORK AND WORK YOUR PLAN"

Put together a "To-do list" of the top ten action items for each day. It can be as simple as putting it down on a piece of paper and keeping it above you on the visor in your car. I use an hour or so on Sunday to put together my top ten list for Monday. Then I review my list at the end of the day and prepare for the next day.

What typically happens as you progress down your list, number two may turn into another appointment because of a referral. Just getting out there and trying to track down leads from other customers many times turns into running into other customers and setting up additional meetings. Cold calling as part of your "top ten list" may turn into appointments, so this list is not just appointments but also cold calls from some of those appointments. You still need to start out with your top ten to do list every day.

"Stop selling. Start helping."

- Zig Ziglar[7]

---

[7] http://www.intenseexperiences.com/motivational-sales-quotes.html

"Chipisms"

> Have you gotten your spiel to the point where it becomes natural and you can actually do it in your sleep?

> Have you perfected your "two-minute elevator speech"?

> Have you developed what I call, "Natural Memorization" of the material you need to present?

> Why is understanding just as important as being able to repeat it to yourself and to the customer?

> What have you implemented from this chapter to start becoming the king of preparation?

> Review the "5 Truths of Sales."

> Put together a "To-do list" of the top ten action items for each day.

> Less is more.

Chapter 6

Perception Is Reality

"Perception is reality. If you are perceived to be something,
you might as well be it because that's the truth
in people's minds."
— **Steve Young**[8]

"When truth is blurred by lies and misinformation, perception becomes reality, and all is lost." What people perceive is usually what they believe, and this is based on what they hear, see, and think. Most of the time we cannot control what happens, but we can always control our reactions.[9]

This is one of the most frustrating "Chipisms" that I have seen in my thirty-two years. Unfortunately, it is true in the corporate world and in any professional setting: "Perception Is Reality." Quite simply, if a boss believes you did something wrong, you did it, even if you believe you did not. It is what it is and that is probably why it is the most frustrating and important "Chipism." It is not fair, but in the real world, you just must accept it, be aware that it happens, and deal with the consequences. You may have to take a step back and say, "Hey, I know I didn't do anything wrong," and then move on. We

---

[8]quotefancy.com/quote/1574889/Steve-Young-Perception-is-reality-If-you-are-perceived-to-be-something-you-might-as-well

[9]https://me.me/i/when-truth-is-blurred-by-lies-and-misinformation-perception-becomes-12567046

all have a story about "perception is reality" and how it has impacted our life.

I explained this important concept to one of my sons when he was being recruited for football. I told him, if you are at a party and you are on one side of the room and your buddy is at the other side of the room and he is doing something like smoking an illegal substance, you are guilty by association even though you are doing nothing wrong. You may not get recruited because of that perception of guilt! It happens all the time. If a person who can impact your career thinks you have done something wrong, you have done it. It is tough to swallow, but it is the way it is in the real world. Certainly, this is one thing in the corporate world that I wish I could change, but I don't think it is ever going to change.

The impact could be you may not get to where you want to go. Your supervisor may not want to put you in a position of leadership. He may not trust you. He may not think you can do it. What is sad is that you know what they say you have done is not true. You know you didn't do it, but it doesn't matter in this world because if they think you did it, you did it.

Innocent until proven guilty does not seem to apply in the real world!

It can hurt you personally, too. You wonder what others are thinking about you. It gets you in your gut. You feel like you've been hit in the stomach. It hurts you so much sometimes that you can become depressed. You are not excited about what you do. You don't come in everyday with a smile on your face. I wish somebody would have told me about "perception is reality" thirty-two years ago. I would have done some things differently had I known about "guilty by association."

What you need to realize if you get caught up in a situation like this is that it will hurt for a while, but in time, you learn to move on and put it behind you. These are just life lessons to learn and understand, but you can't let them change who you are inside. As long as you do things with the right heart and right intent, success will eventually come your way. I just want you to be self-aware and not be blindsided when it happens to you. Everyone, at some point in their career, experiences this lesson! You must understand and discern both the obvious and the behind the scenes things in your environment. You need to listen with your ears, look with your eyes, and speak less with your mouth.

> "Don't take things personally.
> What other people say about you is their reality,
> not yours."
> — **Unknown**[10]

Remember:
The Sun Will Come Up the Next Morning.

Here is another Chipism that follows along this same line of thinking. *A sunrise puts our troubles in perspective.* No matter how dark your life seems right now, a sunrise is waiting on your personal horizon. After thirty-two years in business, nothing in life is that important. Most things can be worked out. Don't worry about things you can't control. There is nothing I have heard in all these years that

---

[10]https://www.pinterest.com/pin/335025659754149399

can't be resolved. Just take a deep breath, get a good night's sleep, and everything will look better the next morning.

Remember the song Little Orphan Annie sang as she sat looking out her window in a deplorable inner-city orphanage? "The sun will come up tomorrow, you can bet your bottom dollar that tomorrow there'll be sun. So ya gotta hang on 'Til tomorrow Come what may."[11]

"The Glass Is Half Full"

"An optimist will tell you the glass is half full;
the pessimist, half empty;
and the engineer will tell you the glass
is twice the size it needs to be."
– Oscar Wilde[12]

People often ask me, what does "The Glass Half Full" mean especially as it relates to sales? "Is the glass half empty or half full?" is a common expression to indicate that a specific situation could be a cause for optimism (half full) or for pessimism (half empty). Most statistics say that if people tend to look at the glass half empty, it is because they are pessimistic by nature. For sure, people who are in a negative mood or negative mindset will look at the glass as half empty. If you do that, it really impacts how you treat people, how you walk around every day, and how you look at things in general.

Positivity breeds positivity,
but negativity breeds negativity.

---

[11]http://www.metrolyrics.com/tomorrow-lyrics-annie.html
[12] http://www.searchquotes.com/search/Half_Full_Half_Empty/#ixzz5EWfp4i98

Personally, I prefer to look at the glass half full. Optimistic people generally have a much more positive outlook on life. I wear a "Stay Positive" band that was designed by a Butler University cancer patient back in 2014. I have worn it now for the last four years, and do not plan on taking it off. It makes a statement when people see it. I love it when they ask me about it.

You see your attitude impacts you every day. It impacts you getting up in the morning. Positive people are looking forward to the day ahead of them. There is so much negativity in this world with everything going on, you really don't want people who look at the glass half empty in your organization. Let me say it in a more of a Chipism way, "Hang out with positive people." They will keep you positive and optimistic. The opposite is also true. Don't hang out with people who are negative because they will bring you down!

Make sure you are one of the positive people who look at the glass half full, so people enjoy hanging out with you.

> "People may hear your words,
> but they feel your attitude."
> **— John C. Maxwell**

**WAYS TO TRAIN YOURSELF TO KEEP A
POSITIVE ATTITUDE AND STAY POSITIVE:**

1) **Exercise Daily** - I use walking, walking with colleagues, and have conference calls while I am walking.

2) **Wear a Stay Positive Band** – It really helps me stay positive which equals a good attitude.

3) **Stay away from gossip/politics in your office.** – This will keep you with a better attitude.

4) **Honor your contract at work.** – This is a way to keep from complaining.

5) **Have a family focus.** Family can be great therapy - My wife keeps me from jumping off bridges and drinking too much.

6) **Control what you can; what you can't control, don't worry about it.**

   "If you keep your feathers well-oiled the water of criticism will run off as from a duck's back."

7) **Hang around positive people with good attitude.** Positivity breeds positivity.

8) **Exude hope. Be an optimist.** Looking at the glass half full means you are optimistic.

9) **Enjoy your work.** Be happy doing what you're doing.

10) **Read some self-help books** and implement what applies to you.

The remarkable thing is we have a choice every day. Life is 10 percent what happens to us and 90 percent how we react to it. I have seen people fired over attitude and not hired over attitude. That is why you need to train yourself to always look at the positive in any situation. Practice on friends, your spouse, your partner, and your mentors. Attitude is something you can control. You choose whether or not you have a good attitude.

Attitude is everything in life.
It can mean the difference between
success and failure.

"If you don't like something, change it.
If you can't change it, change your attitude."
— **Maya Angelou**

"Have a Conversation Not a Presentation."

"The difference between a successful salesperson and a mediocre one often lies in the nuances of social behavior and the skills for building relationships and controlling another person's perception." – Success Magazine[13]

This is by far one of my favorite Chipism's because most people are taught how to present; not how to have a conversation. I am not saying don't learn how to put together a presentation for a meeting; just don't "present it." Too many people get up in front of people as "robots." They want to just present their material with a very monotone voice, lack of facial expressions, and are too scripted. They are not being themselves.

I am not saying it is not a great idea to put slides together for your meeting. Slides are very helpful especially to those who receive information visually better than just verbally. What I am saying is use your slides as a backdrop as you have a "conversation" with your audience.

---

[13] https://www.success.com/article/perception-is-everything

We need to have conversations with people like they are sitting across the table with us, just having a cup of coffee and talking with a close friend. Be relaxed, know your stuff, and bring your personality into the conversation.

Don't monopolize the conversation, either. You need to make sure they get a chance to give you input otherwise you cannot effectively be their problem solver.

"Entering into a conversation with anyone, be it a friend or sales prospect, should resemble a game of backyard catch. Pay attention to how long you hold the ball, and then toss it back in his direction, which signals it's his turn to talk. In time, he'll toss the ball right back to you," says Joe Sweeney, author of *Networking Is a Contact Sport*. "Monopolize conversations and you risk being dismissed as a pompous, full-of-himself bore, even if you're simply overexcited nervously talking to fill awkward silence."

Never assume anything!

As soon as you start assuming, you fall into the trap that you accept everything as truth without checking things out. For example, if you assume the customer saw the marketing material you left at the office or that they remember the last discussions you had, you could be at a big disadvantage when you walk in and immediately start your sales spiel introducing a new product. A big mistake is to assume or take for granted what your customer knows or remembers about you. It is that simple! Always check to see if it really happened before you jump into your conversation/presentation.

"CHIPISMS"

➤ Write out your personal story about "perception is reality."

How has it impacted your life?

➤ Even though it seems unfair, perception is reality in the real world.

Are there things you will do differently now that you know about "guilty by association"?

➤ Attitude is such an important factor in not only your career but your life.

Have you learned to not worry about things you can't control?

Do you consider yourself an optimist or a pessimist?

➤ Review the ways to train yourself to keep a positive attitude and stay positive.

Practice on friends, your spouse, your partner, and your mentors.

➤ There is a difference between giving a presentation and having a conversation with your audience.

Why is it so important to understand and master this concept?

"You Find Mentors; They Do Not Find You."

One of the best ways to perfect the "CHIPISMS" presented in this book is to find mentors that you rely on to lead you, guide you, tell you when you need correction, and praise you when you succeed.

As you have read in my life, mentorship has meant everything to any success I have been blessed to receive. I truly feel I would not be here today if it wasn't for the mentors in my life that helped along the way. Mentors helped me get into dental school, guided me when I discovered dentistry was not the right career for me, and aided me in getting my sales position with Cook Medical.

I cannot emphasize enough how important it is to seek out a mentor or mentors early in life. High school or college is a good place to start to find yourself a mentor. I found one of my mentors in college while I was riding in a bike race. My point is you never know where and when you will run into your mentor. They do not show up on your doorstep. You have to find them through networking and putting your hand out to say hello.

How do you find mentors?

Mentors, for the most part, have years of experience and are wise beyond their years. They should be trustworthy, honest, transparent, and have your best interest at heart.

So, as you begin to look for your mentor, ask yourself:

Does this potential mentor really care about me?
Do they take the time to meet with me on a regular basis?
Do they guide me, helping me discover the right path or choice for me?
Will they be there for me every step of the way?
Do they want to open a door for me to help me implement the advice they are giving me?

That last one is the key! My mentors have always gotten a door open for me, then I had to get the opportunity on my own. By the way, the above list is not multiple choice. You need to find someone who can fulfill all the roles or seek more than one mentor, so all the areas are covered. That does not necessarily mean the same mentor will be with you throughout your entire career either. Sometimes your initial mentor helps you with the first phase of your journey, while a second one picks up and guides you on the next phase.

You find mentors, they do not find you.

My way of finding a mentor in college was through my ability to network. I just walked up to Bill Armstrong, said hello, and began talking to him and building a relationship. Soon, we both knew this was a relationship that was important to pursue.

TIPS TO FINDING A MENTOR:

> Look to a family member, a friend, or a teacher you already know and trust.

> Be willing to meet people; put your hand out and say hello, introduce yourself to all people, especially those with experience and success in the career field you believe you would like to pursue.

> Look for those mentor qualities I described above.

> Remember: The most important quality is do they have your best interest at heart.

You will know when you meet the right person.
It will become obvious because they will want to help you,
guide you, and open doors for you.

Now that you have completed Book One, move on to my second book, "**Bigger Than Sales:** *How Humility and Relationships Build Career Success.*" In this second book, I will give you some very practical steps to follow to become great at sales and love what you are doing along the way to success.

Make a Plan Set Goals, and Implement

Under each list, principle, or Chipism there is space for you to write down what you are doing right now to implement what you have learned or what you will do and when you will do it! Make this a self-inventory evaluating how you are performing and producing now and what you need to do to improve.

Everybody is in Sales!

_____

_____

_____

Identify and implement your passion:

➤ **Step 1:** You must enjoy the art of communication and building relationships with people.

➤ **Step 2:** Figure out what kind of sales you want to go into.

➤ **Step 3**: Is where it gets into your blood and you are having fun.

➤ **Step 4:** You also must have a great work ethic.

79

_____

_____

_____

Sales should be built on relationships that reflect your integrity and good work ethics.

_____

_____

_____

Follow Up + Follow Through = Success

_____

_____

_____

Being on time shows others their time is more valuable to you than yours!

_____

_____

_____

Do what you say you are going to do, and do it when you say you are going to do it!

_____

_____

_____

Listening = Hearing + Understanding (their problem)

_____

_____

_____

"Business Is Always Personal"

☐ "Do the Right Thing."

☐ "Johnny on the Spot."

☐ "Honest as the Day Is Long."

☐ "It's All About People."

☐ "Customers Buy from People They Like."

☐ "Be a Problem Solver."

☐ "Treat People Like You Want to Be Treated."

☐ "Do what you say you are going to do, when you say you are going to do it!"

_____

_____

_____

Success is your own personal responsibility.

Dig deep, take ownership, admit wrong doing, and move on knowing you conquered your fears and take responsibility.

"The Buck Stops Here!"
I believe we should be honest at all costs
and always take personal responsibility
for our actions.

_____

_____

_____

❧ Concentrate on your work and what you can control and let what you can't control roll off your back.

❧ Use self-analysis so you really understand what is going on with your performance.

❧ Be careful with your words, speak less, and listen more. Observe your environment and be more self-aware.

_____

_____

_____

**Learn a few things really well.
I guarantee you will be very successful in sales.
Do you know what to say
in a couple of minutes?**

_____

_____

_____

Follow-up + Follow Through = Success. Quickly get back to your customers and do what you say you are going to do, when you say you are going to do it.

Network. You must learn the art of networking to build your customer base. Get out of your comfort zone and put your hand out to meet people. In my second book, **Bigger Than Sales:** How Humility and Relationships Build Career Success, I share the importance of networking and how to have the right people in it.

Build Positive Relationships. Relationship building is a unique skill you need to develop. Figure out how to relate to people and build the right connections with people and you will build a relationship that is long term, not short term.

Cultivate a Good Attitude. Everything is about attitude and having a positive attitude. How do you react to an unexpected situation? Success breeds success. Negativity breeds negativity. 75-80 percent of your attitude is how you react to a situation. Zig Ziglar's famous quote is, "Your attitude, not your aptitude, will determine your altitude."

Be Passionate about your work, products, and services. Passion is what it is all about. Find your passion and you will not let yourself fail.

_____

_____

_____

Sales is all about Preparation and Repetition.

Repetition is key to learning because most of the skills we need are behavioral in nature.

_____

_____

_____

**Remember:
The Sun Will Come Up the Next Morning.
Positivity breeds positivity,
but negativity breeds negativity.**

_____

_____

_____

Attitude is everything in life. It can mean the difference between success and failure. Attitude determines your altitude!

_____

_____

_____

Never assume anything!

_____

_____

Perception is reality.

**You find mentors, they do not find you.
You will know when you meet the right person.
It will become obvious because they will want
to help you, guide you, and open doors for you.**

List at least three mentors you need to build a relationship with:

Appendix

USE RESOURCES

"LEADERS ARE READERS AND READERS ARE LEADERS."

Those who make time to read bring the following advantages to their life and professional career:

- Better Self-Esteem: They are investing in themselves and feel better about themselves. Why? Because when you're growing, you always feel better about yourself. Reading leadership and sales books helps you to become the best that you can be.

- Creativity and Fresh Ideas: Books always give you new ideas and things to think about.

- Positive Attitude and Healthy Mindset: This is maybe the most important advantage from reading. We live in a negative world with negative thoughts coming at us all the time. You must combat this with putting good thoughts and ideas into your mind.

- Helps in a Competitive Environment: The business world, and especially sales, is extremely competitive. Most people that you compete with do not read on a consistent basis. By reading 10-15 minutes a day, you will set yourself apart from the competition.

- Leadership: If you want to be an effective leader, you have to be a reader. Why? Because you need to be out in front of your people leading and charting the course. Reading gives you those fresh ideas, positive attitude, and perseverance to keep going. The people you lead will pick up on it.

Connect with Chip Helm

Now you really need to get a copy of my book, **Bigger Than Sales:** *How Humility and Relationships Build Career Success.*

To get more of Chip's books, resources,
and materials go to his website:

www.chiphelm.com

To schedule Chip to speak to your sales team, university business class, or business organization, you can contact him at:

Email: chiphelm@nexgenscouting.com

Hear Chip at: https://tinyurl.com/yc3cw6u4

About the Author

From a Dental School drop-out to a National Sales Manager of a multi-billion-dollar medical device company, Chip Helm has honed his sales skills from the ground up. With anecdotal examples from his successes, and failures, Chip's stories will have you laughing while you learn. Chip knows how to develop and maintain long-term relationships to help drive sales success. If it is personal branding, practicing humility, or following-up and following-through, his practical advice is applicable to anyone at any stage in their career. His mentoring, and leadership has helped thousands of students, and colleagues over his last three decades in sales. Chip is a regular guest lecturer at business schools around Indiana, including Purdue, Ball State, Butler University, and Indiana University. He is also a certified coach and college lecturer. His loves are family, work, and his home in Northern Michigan.

Chip holds a BA in Biology from Indiana University and an MBA from the University of South Florida. Married for twenty-six years, Chip met his wife, Cyrilla, at USF while in the MBA program. They have three adult children all pursuing education and professions in health and medical disciplines. Chip has worked for Cook Medical for over thirty-two years.

**"NO MATTER THE CAREER YOU HAVE CHOSEN,
YOU ARE IN SALES."
— Chip Helm**